FOOD

FEASTS, COOKS & KITCHENS

Series Editor:
David Salariya was born in Dundee, Scotland, where he studied illustration and printmaking, concentrating on book design in his post-graduate year. He later completed a further post-graduate course in art education at Sussex University. He has illustrated a wide range of books on botanical, historical and mythical subjects. He has designed and created many new series of children's books for publishers worldwide. In 1989, he established his own publishing company, The Salariya Book Company Ltd.

Author:
Richard Tames is the author of more than fifty books for children, and he has written radio and television programs for schools. He also likes food, especially Indian, Italian and French, Greek, Chinese, Japanese, Spanish...

Consultant:
Jan Metcalfe studied archaeology and has worked for the Science Museum in London for the past thirteen years. She was part of the team that established the *Food For Thought* gallery, which is now a permanent exhibition at the Museum.

Series Editor	David Salariya
Senior Editor	Ruth Nason
Book Editor	Jenny Millington
Consultant	Jan Metcalfe
Artists	Mark Bergin
	Ronald Coleman
	Catherine Constable
	Ryz Hajdul
	John James
	Sarah Kensington
	Mark Peppé
	Carolyn Scrace
	Gerald Wood

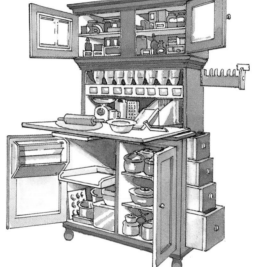

First published in 1994 by Franklin Watts

Franklin Watts
95 Madison Avenue
New York, N.Y. 10016

© The Salariya Book Company Ltd MCMXCIV

Library of Congress Cataloging-in-Publication Data

Tames, Richard.
 Food: feasts, cooks & kitchens / written by Richard Tames. created & designed by David Salariya.
   p. cm. — (Timelines)
 Includes index.
   ISBN 0-531-14312-0 (lib. bdg.) — ISBN 0-531-15711-3 (pbk.)
 1. Food—Juvenile literature. 2. Food habits—Juvenile literature. [1. Food. 2. Food habits.] I. Salariya, David.
II. Title. III. Series: Timelines (Franklin Watts, inc.)
TX355.T36 1993
641.3—dc20
                          93-5675
                          CIP AC

Artists
Mark Bergin, p 18-19, p 22-23; **Ronald Coleman** p 16-17; **Catherine Constable** p 14-15; **Ryz Hajdul** p 12-13, p 38-39; **John James** p 8-9, p 10-11; **Sarah Kensington** p 30-31; **Mark Peppé** p 32-33, p 34-35, p 40-41, p 42-43; **Carolyn Scrace** p 6-7; **Gerald Wood** p 20-21, p 24-25, p 26-27, p 28-29, p 36-37.

Printed in Belgium

TIMELINES
FOOD

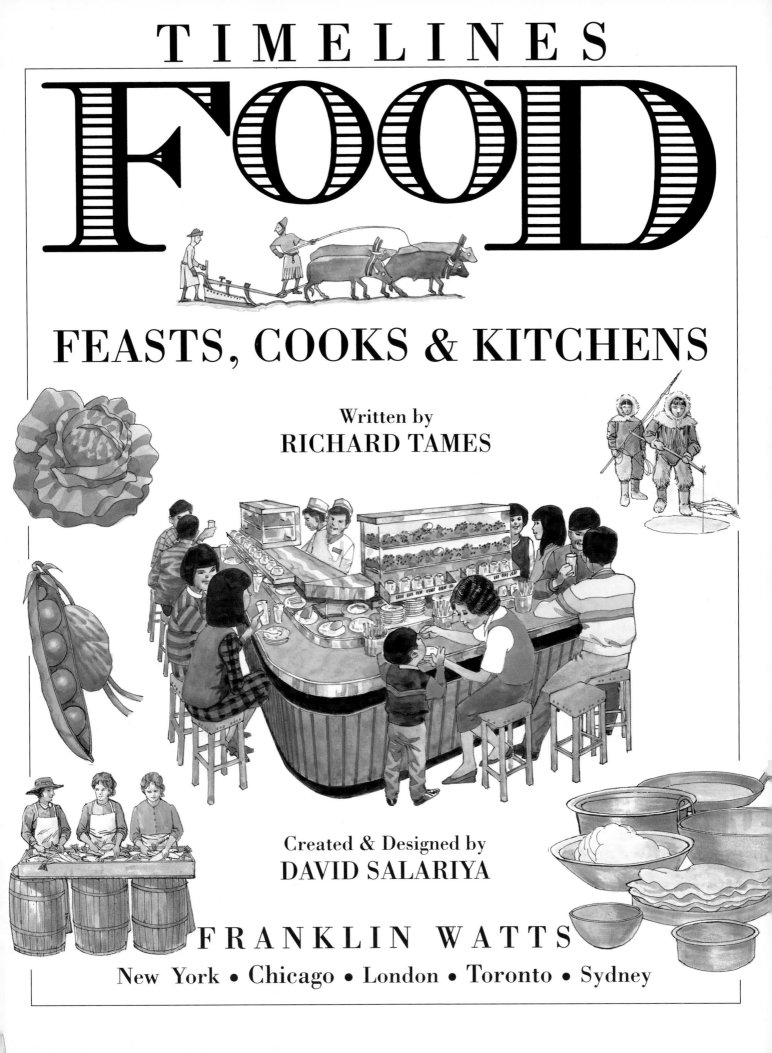

FEASTS, COOKS & KITCHENS

Written by
RICHARD TAMES

Created & Designed by
DAVID SALARIYA

FRANKLIN WATTS
New York • Chicago • London • Toronto • Sydney

CONTENTS

HUNTERS & GATHERERS

BEFORE THE DEVELOPMENT OF FARMING, humans relied on hunting and gathering for their food supply. The hunting-gathering way of life survived into the present century in the Arctic tundra, the Australian desert, and the rain forests of Africa and South America. It requires a large area of land to support even a small population – in the lush rain forest perhaps 5 square miles per person and in the Arctic wastes as much as 500 square miles. Hunter-gatherers usually lived in small groups of up to a few dozen and kept moving on as they used up the food supply in a particular area. Hunting was the task for adult males. Women, old people, and children gathered food – nuts, berries, shellfish, snails, insects, wild honey, and edible fungi, roots, leaves, and seeds. Gathering was almost certainly the more reliable method of getting food, and an expert knowledge of which plants were poisonous would have been important.

△ FOSSIL REMAINS of apes date from about 30,000,000 B.C. Their diet was probably similar to early man's – consisting mainly of nuts, fruits, berries, and leaves.

△ DIGGING FOR TUBERS with a stick. A diet with many roots and nuts in it meant that Neanderthal people needed strong grinding teeth. Fruits were also valued because they were easily gathered and digested.

▷ DANDELIONS were among the many plants eaten. In 1952 the preserved corpse of an iron-age man was found in Denmark. His stomach contained seeds of many plants that we would reject as weeds today.

Dandelion leaves.

Nettles.

Nuts.

◁ HUNTERS catch a woolly mammoth by driving it into a concealed pit. Fish, birds, and small animals were a more regular part of the hunters' food supply.

△ FISH were caught in lakes and rivers. Larger game was left to soften by rotting before being cooked in a pit.

▽ HARDENING the tips of wooden spears in a fire.

▽ HUNTERS made arrow heads by chipping and shaping flint or bone.

▽ THIS DEVICE lengthened the spear-thrower's range against fast-moving animals.

Neolithic sickle.

THE FIRST FARMERS

FARMING EVOLVED as hunter-gatherers used their knowledge of plants to grow and harvest them in a regular and organized way. Farming also meant domesticating animals for their meat, milk, muscle-power, dung, and hides. Changes in the climate may have forced people to settle in one place.

△ THE RIDGES on this pottery tray enabled it to be used as a grater for taking the husks off grain.

△ NEOLITHIC FARMERS cut grain high on the stalk to avoid scattering the seeds. The short sickles were made of bone or of wood set with sharp flints.

▷ THE SUMERIANS lived in what is now Iraq in about 3000 B.C. They domesticated sheep, cattle, goats, and asses. They also dug canals to irrigate their fields.

Because they had to wait to harvest what they had planted, groups now moved on less often. Where there was a regular water supply, settled communities began in the valleys of the Tigris, Nile, Indus, and Yellow rivers. People could live together in much larger groups and because they had a more reliable food supply they had time to learn other skills – making pottery, weaving cloth, and working metal for tools and weapons. As they were no longer living on the move they built more elaborate homes and could have more possessions. The first farming communities emerged in the Middle East, China, and Central America.

△ PEOPLE gave the priests food in return for prayers for a good harvest.

△ AT A SUMERIAN DINNER PARTY the special dishes might include wild boar or any one of 50 kinds of fish. Notice beer being sucked from a jug through a reed drinking tube.

▽ IN MOUNTAINOUS LANDS where rice was the main grain, farmers learned to terrace hills to make fields.

◁ THE MAIN GRAIN in the Americas was maize, or sweetcorn. It was ground up into meal to make porridge, or the kernels were cooked whole in stews.

ANCIENT EGYPT

THE GREEK HISTORIAN Herodotus called Egypt "the gift of the Nile." The annual flooding of the Nile covered the land for miles on each side with a rich layer of silt. An Egyptian noted in 1300 B.C.: "When the Nile overflows the land, the workman has no need to plow. Everybody snores." The Old Testament records that even the slaves who built the pyramids ate well.

△ THE SHADOOF used a simple counterweight to enable the farmer to raise water from one level to another. It is still used today.

△ OVER 90 percent of the people lived within 6 miles (10 km) of the Nile or in the marshy Nile Delta.

Nile water was carried to the fields by canals. Fields nearest the river were the most fertile.

△ BETWEEN July and October the annual flooding of the Nile covered the land with a layer of fertilizing silt.

△ PLOWING and planting followed the annual flooding. Oxen were often used to pull the plow.

△ FIERCE SUMMER TEMPERATURES rose to over 100° F. Hot southerly winds could blow up sandstorms.

△ HARVESTING, around April, meant there was plenty to eat. Food storage was difficult in a hot climate.

△ EGYPTIAN FARMERS used very simple wooden tools. Their plows did not turn the earth very deeply.

Ancient Egyptians pioneered many innovations in the food of the Mediterranean world. By 4000 B.C. they had introduced the watermelon from southern Africa and the fig from Asia Minor (modern Turkey). By 1200 B.C. they were importing cinnamon from Sri Lanka. Egyptians discovered how to preserve meat by dehydrating it, how to hatch eggs by burying them in manure, how to make beer from barley, dates, and water, and how to make cheese.

△ THE SIMPLE BOW-DRILL used friction to start fires for cooking or for heating the clay bread ovens.

△ COOKING A GOOSE over a fire. Geese were valued for their eggs and feathers as well as for their meat. This must have been a special occasion; bread and vegetables made up the bulk of most people's daily diet, with hardly any meat.

△ BEEHIVES made of clay existed by 2500 B.C. Honey was the main sweetener in cooking.

△ SLAUGHTERING an ox. The horns and hide were as valued as the meat. Most people relied on fish or poultry for protein.

▷ FEASTS were held at religious festivals. Egyptians ate boiled cabbage to avoid being sick from drinking too much wine.

△ A GREEK HUNTER with his dog. Mountainous, dry Greece had much less game (wild animals and birds) than northern Europe.

▽ OUR WORD "symposium" – a learned conference – comes from the Greek word for a drinking party.

ANCIENT GREECE

THE ANCIENT GREEKS lived on a rather plain diet. A typical meal might consist of flat barley bread made without yeast, a salad dressed with basil or parsley, cheese, olives, and figs, washed down with a thick wine diluted with water. Very poor people ate unappetizing foods such as turnips and grasshoppers. Modern Greek cooking still features olives, flat bread, goat's milk cheese, and wine flavored with resin.

△ WOMEN pounding grain into flour. The Greeks grew barley but also ate white bread made from imported wheat.

▽ DIONYSUS was the Greek god of wine. The Greeks mixed wine with honey or resin to flavor and preserve it.

◁ GREEK WINE was famed for its strength and flavor. It was a major export, exchanged for spices.

▽ AN OLIVE PRESS extracts the oil from ripe olives.

While most ordinary Greeks ate simple food, the people of wealthy cities like Athens could afford imported luxuries like almonds, rice, and spices. The warrior-nation of Spartans lived on a famous "black broth" made from pork stock, vinegar, and salt. One Athenian wit claimed this bitter brew was the cause of Spartan bravery – even death was better than having to eat such awful stuff.

▽ THIS FRIEZE shows a procession going to sacrifice oxen to the gods to ensure a good harvest.

△ THE GREEK CLIMATE favored olives and vines as main crops. Olive oil was used for cooking,

and for making soap and cosmetics. It was also useful as a fuel to burn in lamps.

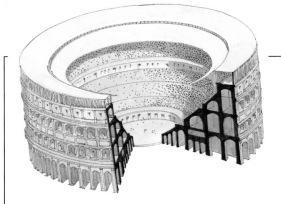

△ ROMAN EMPERORS had to keep the poor happy by giving them free bread and circus shows with gladiators.

By A.D. 270, many Romans were getting free bread and sometimes rations of pork fat and olive oil.

ANCIENT ROME

AT THE HEIGHT of the Roman Empire, the city of Rome had a population of one million. Grain to feed the people was brought from Egypt and Sicily, and the boats bringing it were forbidden to stop anywhere on their voyage. Some foodstuffs, common in other times and places, never became a regular part of the Roman diet. Butter was used only as a medicine and milk as a cosmetic. Rice, sugar, and carrots were rarely used.

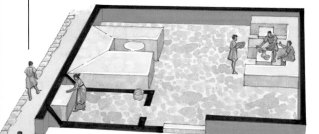

◁ △ MANY POOR ROMANS lived in apartment blocks without kitchens. They had to eat in taverns like these, which sold snacks. The counters had special holes for jars that kept food hot.

▽ FRUIT AND VEGETABLES made up a large part of the Roman diet. Figs, olives, and leeks were popular with the poor.

▽ A ROMAN BUTCHER. Pork was the most common meat. Useful animals like oxen were not killed for food.

△ BECAUSE bread was the staple food, bakeries needed to produce it on a large scale. Donkey-powered mills ground grain into flour. Big ovens could bake 80 loaves at once. Bakers also made cakes flavored with honey, cheese, or pepper.

◁ KITCHENS had a brick oven and sink. Pans, ladles, and strainers were made of bronze, jugs and plates of earthenware.

▽ ORDINARY PEOPLE ate flat, hard barley bread. Soldiers were given a diet of this as a punishment. Poor Romans filled themselves with bread and thick soup of barley with beans. Water was the usual drink, or sometimes vinegary wine.

▷ A ROMAN DINNER PARTY usually had nine guests. They reclined on couches set out in a U-shape around the table. Slaves would entertain the guests with music and singing, and sometimes there would also be clowns or dancers. The guests brought their own napkins to wrap any leftover food and take it home.

Rich Romans gave fabulous banquets to display their great wealth. The dishes they served contained expensive ingredients brought from the far corners of the empire and beyond – oysters from Britain, ham from France, wine from Greece, prawn sauce from Spain, pepper from India, and ginger from China. The Roman writer Petronius described a show-off host who tried to impress his guests by serving dormice rolled in honey and poppyseeds, and a sow stuffed with live thrushes (to fly out when it was cut open). Even normal recipes required lots of highly flavored ingredients, especially pepper and a fish sauce, liquamen, made from fermented anchovies. Wines were also very strong and usually drunk diluted with water.

Some Romans ate so much that they had their houses fitted with a vomitorium – a sort of marble-lined drain where, helped by a slave poking his fingers down their throat, they could throw up what they had eaten and then go back to the feast and start again.

▷ RICH ROMANS could afford colored glass goblets or shiny red pottery called Samian ware which was made in factories in Italy and France.

▽ FISH SAUCE, OR LIQUAMEN, was an important part of a Roman dinner party. The main dish usually consisted of roasted meat with liquamen, pepper, and oil poured over it. A recipe for liquamen is illustrated below.

| The sprats or anchovies are crushed. | They are mixed with the intestines of larger fish. | The mixture is left in the sun to mature. | The liquamen is strained off the fish mixture. |

△ A ROMAN spoon and soup ladle.

▷ SOLDIERS catered for themselves, using army-issue spits, grids, portable ovens, and handmills.

THE DARK AGES

DURING THE EARLY MIDDLE AGES most of Europe was covered by dense forest that was rich in game but no friend to the farmer. In England the Anglo-Saxons cleared the land with axe and fire, and used massive eight-ox plow-teams to work the heavy clay soils. Meanwhile, on the fringes of Europe, other peoples worked out ways of living that depended on herding, hunting, or fishing, rather than farming. The areas they inhabited had poor soils or were too mountainous, too cold, or too dry to support agriculture on a large scale. The diet of these peoples tended to be rich in meat, fish, or dairy products, but poor in vegetables and fruit, except nuts or berries. As fuel was often scarce, much of their food was smoked, dried, or fermented to make it palatable – or simply eaten raw. Grains and spices for a more varied diet could be obtained by trading.

△ AT FEASTS Anglo-Saxons drank ale or mead, made from honey, out of huge ox horns or wooden pots.

▽ THE MILK of camels, yaks, and sheep was made into butter, curds, and yogurt. Animals were not killed for food, but eaten when they died.

◁ IN SCANDINAVIA, the Vikings used elaborate cooking utensils. The Viking diet relied heavily on mutton, reindeer, birds, bear, and shellfish.

▽ AN INUIT WOMAN uses a rib bone to get the rich marrow from a caribou's anklebone. Intense cold will keep the meat from spoiling.

◁ CENTRAL ASIAN nomads have traditionally lived on the blood and milk of their herds as much as on their meat.

△ CARIBOU MEAT being sliced for wind-drying on a rack.

Perhaps surprisingly a number of these traditional ways of life have survived into the twentieth century. Lapps still run huge herds of reindeer in northern Scandinavia and the descendants of the Mongols still roam the steppes of central Asia. The Inuit peoples of the Arctic regions have exchanged the spear and bow for the rifle but still use the kayak (a light wooden one-person canoe, covered with sealskin) for transportation.

▷ *Circassian chicken.*

MIDDLE EASTERN FOOD

THE RELIGION OF ISLAM spread through the Middle East in the 7th and 8th centuries. Its followers are called Muslims. Like the Jews, Muslims are forbidden by their religion to eat pig meat. Like Jews also they are required to eat only meat which has been ritually slaughtered and drained of its blood. During the month of Ramadan Muslims are obliged to fast from dawn until dusk. The very old, the very young, the sick, and travelers are exempted from fasting.

▷ CIRCASSIANS, a Muslim people of southern Russia, gave their name to this spicy chicken dish.

▷ ALL ARAB PEOPLES have inherited from the desert Bedouin a tradition of warm hospitality to travelers and especially to pilgrims. Flat bread like this is often shared with guests.

▷ A TRADITIONAL Turkish *lokanta* (restaurant) offers entertainment as well as refreshment to the tired traveler. The barrels and flasks suggest that the strict Muslim ban on alcohol is being ignored.

Lying at the junction of three continents, the Middle Eastern countries controlled trade in spices for centuries. Skill in combining different spices is a feature of Middle Eastern cooking. Another is the use of sweet ingredients, such as dates, honey, almonds, or apricots, in combination with meat and other savory items. Middle Eastern cooking draws on the traditions of the Turks, Persians, and Berbers of North Africa. Mutton is the most widely favored meat. Cooking in milk, yogurt, or rosewater is common. Staple foods include rice, flat bread, cracked wheat (bulgur), and a sort of semolina used for making couscous, a traditional dish from North Africa. Middle Eastern foods now popular in the West include kebabs, moussaka, and "Turkish Delight."

△ IN MUSLIM COUNTRIES it has been traditional to eat using only the right hand, which is therefore kept especially clean. Sharing food from a common plate also requires consideration for other diners and especially for guests. Usually diners sit on the floor, having removed their shoes.

◁ THIS STUNNING PLATE was made at Iznik in Turkey. Blue and white ware was at first copied from Chinese models, but Turkish craftsmen then added green and red. Tulips and carnations were favorite motifs.

△ MUSLIM BANQUETS were enhanced by fine tableware like this Egyptian ewer made of bronze and a jug carved from a solid piece of rock crystal.

▽ IN ARAB COUNTRIES, men often prepare the coffee.

CHINA

△ THE KITCHEN of a wealthy household of around 200 A.D. Rich people enjoyed such delicacies as stewed turtle, spiced tortoise, casseroled duck, honey fritters, and over 50 different varieties of rice.

△ A 2ND-CENTURY TOMB-TILE from Sichuan shows diners kneeling at low tables. There is a bowl of soup and a serving spoon in the foreground.

DESPITE ITS IMMENSE VARIETY Chinese cooking has had basic common features for at least 3,000 years. Chopsticks are not only used for eating with but in the kitchen take the place of whisks and spoons. Dishes are classified into "Five Flavors" – bitter, salt, hot, sweet, and sour – which are combined for contrast and balance.

Meals consist of a grain to provide bulk (*fan*) and "small eats" (*sung*) to give flavor. The grain may be boiled rice, millet porridge, or wheat made into noodles or dumplings. The side dishes consist of vegetables, especially greens and gourds, fish, and small amounts of thinly sliced meat, usually pork. The most common cooking methods are boiling, steaming, and stir-frying.

◁ THE TEAHOUSE has long been a place for gossip and doing business over a drink and snack.

▷ THE LYCHEE has been cultivated for its sweet flesh for over 2,000 years.

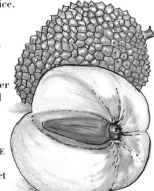

SONG DYNASTY SALAD

Stir-fry some thin strips of bacon and leave to cool. Mix matchstick-sized pieces of pickled cucumbers and radishes with crushed garlic and shredded tangerine peel. Add the meat and serve as a side-dish.

△ THE STEEP-SIDED metal wok is used for stir-frying, simmering, and deep-fat frying.

◁ ONE CHOPSTICK is held still with thumb and ring finger, the other one with thumb and first two fingers.

▽ NOODLES, a Chinese invention, were eaten only by the poor until about 1500.

▷ A SELECTION OF DIM SUM – portions of meat, shrimp, or vegetables wrapped in thin pastry or edible leaves. They are served with sauces and dips.

◁ THIS 19TH-CENTURY
PAINTING shows tea being packed into
jars. Tea was introduced to Japan from
China in the 9th century.

JAPAN

A BASIC JAPANESE MEAL has long consisted of *ichiju sansai* – "soup and three." First comes *miso* (fermented bean paste) soup, which is eaten by almost every Japanese almost every day. Then come a portion of fresh, raw fish, a grilled dish, and a simmered dish. All these are served in separate bowls because Japanese insist on elegant presentation. They are accompanied by boiled, sticky rice (easier to pick up with chopsticks), green tea (without milk or sugar), and sharp, tangy pickles. The traditional Japanese diet is low in fat and very healthy.

△ THE EQUIPMENT
needed for a formal
Japanese ceremony,
which can last for
hours.

FRIED SQUID

Dry some rings of squid
in a pan in the oven. Toss
them in flour, and fry
with some onion rings.
Serve with a sauce of
garlic, crushed, toasted
breadcrumbs, and
vinegar.

▷ SUSHI are snacks
made from vinegared
rice topped with freshly
caught fish, shellfish, or
omelet.

◁ TOFU, a curd made
from soybeans, is high
in protein but low in
calories.

◁ THESE
traditional
candies are
shaped like
cherry blossoms
and a maple leaf.

△ A TIGHTLY PACKED
O-bento – lunch box –
can be bought at any
large railroad station.

▽ A PLATTER OF SUSHI in the style of the Edo
period (1603-1868). This may be eaten as a one-
course lunch or served instead
of canapés at a party
or reception.

Over the last century Japan's increasing trade with other countries has led to some new foods being eaten; but these have added to, rather than displacing, the basic pattern of rice, fish, and pickles. Meat is now much more commonly eaten, as are dairy products. Foreign contacts have led to influences both ways. Instant "pot noodles" are a Japanese invention. The beautiful presentation of "nouvelle cuisine" was basically inspired by Japanese traditions.

SALT

SALT IS ESSENTIAL FOR LIFE. Hunting peoples get it directly from raw or roast meat, but people living on boiled meat or cereals must add it to their diet. For centuries salt was used to preserve fish and meat. Without salted food, the great navigators could never have made the voyages that created world trade.

△ THE ROAD linking Rome with the salt pans at Ostia, on the coast, was called the Via Salaria – the Salt Road. Roman soldiers got money – a *salarium* – to buy salt rations. This is where our word "salary" comes from.

△ THE GREAT ITALIAN TRADING CITY of Venice first grew rich from salt, made in the lagoons which surround it. Later it became a major center for handling spices from the East.

△ THIS FABULOUS GOLD SALTCELLAR was made by the Italian craftsman Benvenuto Cellini for King Francis I of France. For centuries the *gabelle* (salt tax) provided French kings with a major source of revenue. Hatred of this tax helped cause the revolution of 1789.

▽ SLABS OF SALT have been used as a currency in desert areas of Africa for centuries.

△ A CARAVAN of camels carrying slabs of salt across the great Sahara desert. The salt is pried from ancient seabeds and cut to shape.

Salt has some 14,000 uses, more than any other mineral. It is used to freeze ice cream, soften water, tan leather, and make such products as bread, cheese, glass, soap, batteries, and rocket fuel. Salt manufacture is one of the world's oldest industries. The mines at Hallstatt, near Salzburg (Salt Town) in Austria, have been worked since the early Iron Age. Salt has also been used as a symbol of health and hospitality throughout the world.

◁ IN 1930, INDIAN LEADER Gandhi marched to the sea to make salt, as a protest against the salt tax imposed by India's British rulers.

Ginger.

△ THE UNDERGROUND STEM of the ginger plant is used to flavor candy and pastries in Europe and meat in India.

Nutmeg.

Mace.

△▽ MACE is the outer layer of the nutmeg, the seed of an evergreen tree from the Molucca Islands. Cardamom is also a seed.

Cardamom.

Cinnamon.

SPICE

SPICES WERE REGULARLY TRADED between Asia and Europe at least as early as 500 B.C. Most went overland but one route used a 4000-mile canoe voyage from Indonesia to Africa, land carriage north, then another voyage across the Red Sea, followed by camel caravan across the Middle East. Spices were used as gifts between kings, and were often kept under lock and key. The Crusades increased the taste for spicy food in Europe, and Venice grew rich from a trade which linked countries as distant as Scotland and China. By 1400 there were three huge shipments of spices from India each year, mostly of pepper and ginger.

△ CINNAMON, the bark of a tropical tree, is used to flavor wine, soups, meat, and pastries.

Garlic.

△ GARLIC has been used as a medicine and to ward off plague, devils, and vampires.

◁ ONE POUND of saffron requires the stigmas of 70,000 crocus flowers, picked the same day.

Saffron.

◁▽ TRADE in spices enriched the Arab world which joins Europe to Africa and Asia.

After 1400 the Portuguese broke the Venetian stranglehold on the spice trade by sailing around Africa to India. They were later challenged by the Dutch, who took over Indonesia and then the British who took over India. One of the reasons Christopher Columbus sailed west was to find a new route to China and help Spain break into the spice trade. He never reached China but instead found a New World – and new spices, like the chili pepper, which he brought back to Europe.

△ HIGH-VALUE TRADE. This solid gold letter was written in 1620 from the Nayak of Tanjore to the King of Denmark. For 18 iron cannon, the Danes bought the right to build a fort at Tranquebar on the southern coast of India and buy pepper locally for export to Europe. In 1845 the Danes sold the port to the British.

▽ PEPPERCORNS were ideal for trade – low in bulk, but high in value.

▷ TRADE with America brought new spices like hot chili peppers and the fragrant pods of the vanilla plant.

Chili powder.

Chili peppers.

Peppercorns.

Vanilla pods.

△ THE BAYEUX TAPESTRY shows Norman cooks boiling food in a big cauldron, baking cakes, and serving food on spits.

THE MIDDLE AGES

△ COOKING was often done outdoors to cut down the risk of fire. The knights have made a table by laying their shields on trestles. Table manners were rather rough, even among nobles. Leftovers were thrown on the floor for the dogs.

△ PIES were often very richly decorated

MEDIEVAL LIFE was ruled by the Church. Christians were told not to eat meat on Wednesdays, Fridays, and Saturdays, during the six weeks of Lent or on other holy days. In all, about half the days in the year were supposed to be meatless days. Chicken and other poultry were not always classified as meat. But at other times even cheese was forbidden. Sick people and children were exempted from these rules. On fast days the regular substitute for meat was fish. Monasteries kept large fish ponds called "stews" to ensure a regular supply.

◁ MEDIEVAL COOKS not only used herbs familiar to us, like parsley and borage, but also violets and primroses.

Parsley.

Borage.

△ HUNTING for hares around 1400. The hunt supplied game for the table, and riding and shooting were also good training for war.

◁ MONASTERIES often cared for the sick and so had special gardens to grow herbs for medicines. Thyme and rosemary were especially valued. Here monks are shown preparing medicines.

▽ PICTURES drawn in the margins of a psalm book belonging to the 14th-century Luttrell family show the farmer's tasks through the year. Note the use of oxen, rather than horses, for plowing heavy land.

△ A BAKER who sold underweight bread is publicly punished.

Shortage of winter fodder was a major problem in the medieval village. Because it was impossible to feed all the animals through the winter, the weaker ones were slaughtered each autumn and the meat salted or smoked to preserve it. Early spring was a time of hardship with stores of last season's food running low and preserved meat in danger of going bad and causing disease. Peasants mostly ate coarse bread and "pottage," a thick soup in which onions, cabbage, and broad beans were boiled up with herbs and perhaps a little pork or bacon. Their pigs were fed on kitchen waste.

△ THIS 15TH-CENTURY PICTURE shows a baker making rolls. An assistant is baking pies.

▷ EUROPEANS first saw windmills in the Middle East during the Crusades. Before that they had only water-powered mills or "quern stones" to grind grain by hand.

△ A RICH LORD'S KITCHEN, c.1350. Note the serving men, dressed in livery, lining up for dishes to carry through to the hall. By the open fire (right) a boy is turning the spit.

△ THE HARE, much bigger than the rabbit, yielded not only more meat but also fur which could be used to trim a hunting cloak. Poaching was severely punished by cutting off the poacher's fingers or feet, to prevent him from offending again.

△ KING JOHN of Portugal feasts the English prince, John of Gaunt. They eat from trenchers — stale bread used as plates. At the end of the meal the trenchers are also eaten.

▽ FARM WORK occupied 90 percent of the population in medieval times. Even townspeople came out to the fields to help when the harvest had to be brought in.

△ MEDIEVAL MILLS were much smaller and flimsier than the ones still seen today.

BACON & PEA SOUP

Boil some dried peas in bacon stock with an onion and a bay leaf for 1½ hours. Take out the bay leaf and mash the peas thoroughly. Stir in some diced cooked ham or bacon, boil the soup again and serve.

THE RENAISSANCE

◁ FORKS came from Turkey to Italy in the 14th century.

RENAISSANCE ITALY set new standards of elegance in the arts of cooking and eating. Forks, napkins, and tablecloths came into more common use. The invention of printing made it possible to produce gardening manuals, herbals, and cookbooks on a large scale.

◁ RENAISSANCE GOBLETS.

▽ AN ITALIAN KITCHEN of c.1400. Lavish entertaining needed lots of servants.

An oil lamp.

Water taps.

A sugar-loaf.

Bread oven.

Mixing dough.

Making pasta.

Lining a pie dish.

◁ A PIE-MAKER sharing a shop with a butcher c.1450. Most of the butcher's leftover scraps probably ended up in the pies, disguised with spices.

▷ THE TURKEY came to Europe from Mexico via Spain. Merchants trading with the Middle East brought it into England – hence the name – "turkey."

◁ AN AZTEC MOTHER watches her daughter make tortillas – still a Mexican favorite.

▽ EUROPE'S SEALINK with the Americas brought many new foods.

Kidney beans.

Potatoes.

Pineapple.

Tomatoes.   Cocoa beans.

Spain was the main gateway for introducing "New World" plants like peppers, maize, and peanuts to the rest of Europe. The recipe for preparing drinking chocolate from cocoa, sugar, cinnamon, and vanilla was guarded as a Spanish state secret.

In Protestant countries, "meatless" days were no longer required by religion, but fish-eating was still encouraged so that sailors needed in war could find jobs as fishermen in peacetime.

The Spanish learned about potatoes from the Incas of Peru, who lived too high in the cold Andes mountains to grow maize. The potato soon became a staple food in Spain and Ireland but it took over two centuries to be accepted in France and Germany. It was not grown in North America until it was introduced from Europe in 1719. An English recipe book of the 16th century recommended eating potatoes with butter, pepper, oil, vinegar, salt, sugar, or the juice of oranges or lemons. Europeans introduced "New World" maize to Africa, and took peanuts, sweet potatoes, lima beans, chili peppers, and tobacco to China.

▽ THE SEEDS of the sunflower, introduced from America, can be dried and chewed, or crushed to yield an oil used in cooking. The "Jerusalem Artichoke" is really a sunflower with edible roots.

▷ A FRENCH pastry maker of the 17th century. Once sugar became much cheaper, it could be used to make elaborate decorations on cakes and as an ingredient in the first candies, such as marzipan, a paste of sugar and ground almonds.

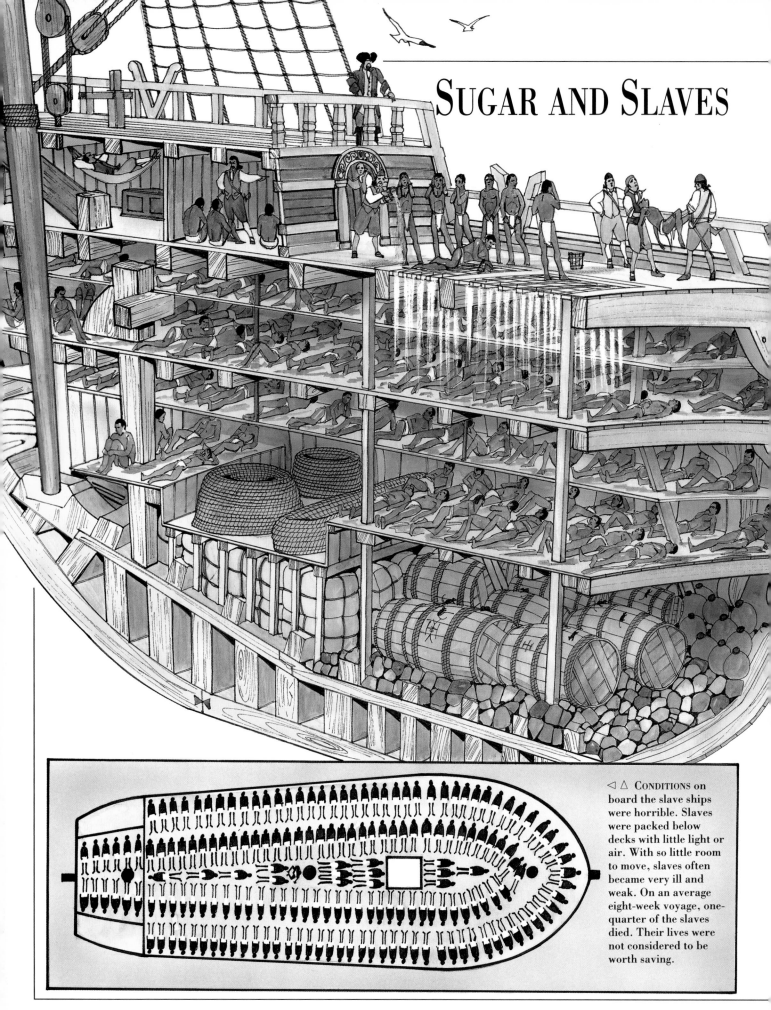

◁ △ CONDITIONS on board the slave ships were horrible. Slaves were packed below decks with little light or air. With so little room to move, slaves often became very ill and weak. On an average eight-week voyage, one-quarter of the slaves died. Their lives were not considered to be worth saving.

△ ALMOST ALL SLAVES were Africans. Whole families might be bought, split up, and sold off separately. It was common to brand them like animals. Whipping was a common punishment for trying to escape. Slaves spoke different languages, so it was difficult for them to unite and revolt.

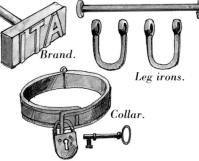

▷ COLLARS and leg irons prevented slaves from escaping. Brand-marks were proof of "ownership."

Brand.

Leg irons.

Collar.

THE "NEW WORLD" of the Americas had a suitable climate for growing sugarcane, which was brought to Hispaniola (Haiti) from Europe by Christopher Columbus in 1493. It was in Brazil that sugar first became big business. The Portuguese controlled both this huge country and the trade with western Africa, from where they took black slaves to provide the labor they needed. In 1550 there were five sugar plantations in Brazil; by 1623 there were 350. Large mills were built to crush the juice out of the cane. This was then boiled to make crystals which were set in cone-shaped "loaves." There was a demand for sugar in Europe to sweeten the fashionable new drinks of tea, coffee, and chocolate and, by about 1730, to make jam too.

◁ A "SCRAMBLE" slave auction in Brazil. Buyers paid a fixed price per slave and then rushed to grab the best ones after a gun was fired as a starting signal.

North America.

South America.

Europe.

Africa.

△ THE SLAVE TRADE was part of a triangle taking guns and cloth to Africa and sugar back to Europe.

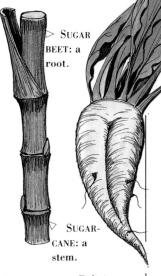

▷ SUGAR BEET: a root.

▽ SUGAR-CANE: a stem.

▽ SLAVES AT WORK, processing sugarcane. Religious reformers campaigned to end slavery. It was abolished in the British Empire in 1833, in the United States in 1863, and in Brazil in 1889. By then about 20,000,000 Africans had been taken across the Atlantic, most of them to work on sugar plantations.

In Britain the average consumption of sugar tripled between 1700 (4 lbs per person per year) and 1780 (12 lbs). Sugar-growing lands were prized above all other colonies and were often fought over. The French agreed to surrender the whole of Canada so that they could keep the West Indian island of Guadeloupe. The Dutch gave up New York for Suriname in South America.

EAST INDIAMEN

BETWEEN 1600 AND 1800 the Dutch and the British replaced the Portuguese as masters of the trade between Europe and Asia. Both countries had an "East India Company" specializing in this trade. The Dutch controlled exports from Japan, Indonesia, and Sri Lanka, the British from India. All the main European powers struggled for a share of the trade with China. The spice trade continued to be highly profitable, especially for the Dutch, whose hold on Indonesia gave them the best source of cloves, mace, and nutmeg. But even the spice trade was overshadowed by two new commodities – tea and coffee, which were first sold in England in 1657. Tea was drunk Chinese-style, without milk and sugar, from small bowls without handles. In 1700, Britain imported 20,000 pounds of tea – a century later, 20,000,000 pounds. The Dutch and other Europeans preferred coffee to tea. Coffee is native to Africa and was first seen by Europeans in the Middle East. By 1720, the Dutch had found that they could grow it in Indonesia. Later they grew it in Sri Lanka and the British took it to the West Indies. Today, half the world's coffee comes from Brazil.

△ AN "EAST INDIAMAN" being loaded. These 3-masted ships ranged from 400 to 1,500 tons and were armed against pirates.

△ CHINESE TEA being packed into chests. It was vital to keep the tea absolutely dry on the long voyage to Europe. If it got wet, the precious cargo was useless.

▽ TRADING STATIONS leased by different countries lined the banks of the Pearl River, just outside Canton in China.

△ CAPTAIN TONDER, who began Denmark's trade with China in 1731, was given this small pottery portrait of himself by the Chinese.

△ A RETURNED SAILOR shows off a cockatoo. Sailors often brought home unusual souvenirs.

On long voyages to Asia, sailors lived on hard biscuit and salted meat. Lack of vegetables and fresh fruit led to swollen legs and rotten gums and could be fatal. This was scurvy, a disease first accurately described in 1612 by the Surgeon General of the Dutch East India Company. In 1734, a Dutch doctor, Johannnes Bachstromm, showed that it was caused by a lack of fresh fruit and vegetables. A Scottish navy doctor, James Lind, advised Captain James Cook to carry citrus fruit (oranges, lemons, and limes) on his voyage to Australia. None of his crew died from scurvy, although they were away for three years. By 1800 scurvy was almost unknown in the Royal Navy as sailors had lime juice mixed in with their daily rum ration.

△ A PLATE made in China in 1850 for export to Britain.

▽ MERCHANTS gather in the courtyard of East India House in Amsterdam in the late 1700s.

AFRICA

AFRICAN DISHES often consist of two basic elements: a starchy bulk food (yam, cassava, sweet potato, plantain) or a cereal (rice, sorghum, millet); and a thick sauce or stew of vegetables (spinach, okra, tomatoes) with meat or fish or nuts. Cheese, salads, and raw vegetables are not part of traditional cuisine but there are many types of soups and drinks made from fruits. Most cooking is over an open wood fire.

△ AMONG NOMADS, like the Fulani of West Africa, large herds are a sign of wealth.

However, having many cattle is a disadvantage if there is a shortage of fodder. None of the animals yields as much milk as it should.

△ THE YAM is a tropical climbing plant which produces a starchy edible tuber. Yam tubers can weigh as much as 100 lbs (45 kgs).

SESAME RICE

Boil 600ml of milk, add 1½ oz of rice and boil for 2 hours. Toast and crush some sesame seeds. Add them to the rice with some honey.

△ THE FLESH and milk of the coconut are widely used as a seasoning or a basic ingredient.

African specialities depend on local resources. The national dish of Eritrea is mutton with pimiento paste, while Madagascar's is a stew of zebra with tomatoes and ginger, and the Ivory Coast has cockerel fried in palm oil. Other delicacies include viper stew in Cameroon, camel with yams in Mali, and monkey kebabs in Senegal.

▽ AFRICAN SNAILS are a delicacy, and can grow up to four times as big as European ones.

△ IN MANY West African markets most of the stall-holders are women.

△ ▷ OKRA and bananas both grow in West Africa.

▷ SORGHUM can feed both humans and animals. It is used to make porridge or flat cakes. In Mali it is used for couscous and in Sudan for making beer.

INDIA

IN INDIA, FOOD AND RELIGION are closely connected. For Hindus, the cow is sacred and should not be killed – but far more people can be fed from a live cow than from the carcass of a dead one. Milk can be drunk, or mixed with grain to make gruel. The sharp taste of curds is very refreshing in hot weather. Butter is heated to make *ghee*, which is widely used for cooking and will keep for months, even in a tropical climate.

About 500 years ago, India was conquered by the Mughals, who were Muslims. They brought with them new dishes like kebabs (spicy cubes of meat grilled on skewers), pilau (rice with shredded chicken), and candies made out of flour, sugar, honey, and spices.

When the British ruled India, between 1857 and 1947, they learned to eat curry and other Indian dishes such as kedgeree (a spicy mixture of rice and fish), mulligatawny (a hot curry soup whose name meant "pepper-water"), and chutneys (spicy vegetable and fruit pickles).

GEELI KHICHRI

Boil some mung beans and ginger slices together for about 1½ hours until the beans are soft. Take out the ginger and add some cumin seeds. Mash the beans and serve.

△ RICE, native to India, has been grown in irrigated paddy-fields for centuries.

THE MUGHAL ▽ EMPEROR Babur, who lived from 1483 to 1530, enjoys a feast.

△ THE MASKED SERVANTS in this Hindu kitchen show a traditional concern for "purity" – which is not quite the same as hygiene. Hindu ideas of purity required the use of brass bowls (*below*), which could be scoured with ashes, rather than absorbent pottery.

▽ A ROADSIDE candy peddler. Indians knew how to get sugar from sugarcane by 500 B.C.

◁ NOT ALL CURRIES use hot chili peppers but India is the world's largest spice producer.

▷ A REAL Indian "take-out." "Tiffin" (lunch) is still delivered in tiered metal containers today.

KITCHEN TO TABLE

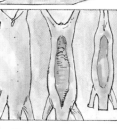

UNLIKE ARISTOCRATS in France or Germany, English landowners spent very little time at court or in the capital unless they had business there. Most lived on their estate and took a real interest in how it was run. It was therefore in the country that they entertained guests; and a big part of the entertainment was a meal of the best produce the estate could provide. Each estate might specialize in either cultivation or dairy farming, but the "home farm" that actually served the owner's own house was often run to provide all the household needs in the way of meat, milk, eggs, fruit, and vegetables.

△ ROOT VEGETABLES, such as carrots, rutabagas, and turnips, could be kept for months if stored in fine sand in a dry place.

△ HOME-SLAUGHTERED PIGS or sheep provided not only joints of meat but offal, blood, and scraps to make sausages and pies.

△ A WALLED kitchen garden with its own greenhouse and vine-house could provide everyday vegetables, such as beans and greens, herbs, soft fruits (blackcurrants, gooseberries, raspberries), and even sweet peppers, peaches, and pineapples, which needed artificial heating and much skill and attention.

△ VEGETABLES were usually washed clean before being brought to the kitchen for preparation.

△ THE COOK was supreme in the kitchen. She gave orders to the others and made the most difficult dishes.

△ A VICTORIAN RECIPE for mutton cutlets. Dip cutlets in egg and coat in breadcrumbs and chopped ham.

Fry the cutlets on both sides so that the meat is cooked right through and the outside of each cutlet is crisp.

Make "reform chips" by mixing 1/2-inch strips of carrots, black truffles, ham, gherkins, and white of boiled egg.

Serve the cutlets and "reform chips" with "reform sauce" – made with eighteen different ingredients!

△ THE SCULLERY MAID did the dishwashing with "washing soda," that left her hands very sore.

▷ EVEN an informal meal might have five or six courses, each one requiring separate cutlery and a clean glass for the wine which accompanied it.

After the arrival of the railroads in the mid-1800s, the weekend "country house party" became common among the upper classes in England. The day would begin with a hearty cooked breakfast, including such special dishes as deviled kidneys or kedgeree. Because guests passed the daytime outdoors, shooting or playing tennis or croquet, lunch was not such a heavy meal or might even be a picnic. In the summer, tea with cakes and sandwiches would be served on the lawn. At dusk guests would return to the house to change into formal evening clothes for a lavish dinner. This was an opportunity for the host and hostess to show off not only their elegant silverware and fine wines, but also the skills of their gardeners and cooks in being able to create a superb meal. The production of all this food required a small army of servants working behind the scenes from dawn till midnight. The great days of this style of living ended with World War I, but the modern "country house" hotel tries to recreate its atmosphere by giving guests individual attention and using the freshest local produce in its restaurant.

A MENU FOR DINNER
1890
Cressy Soup
Boiled haddock
with egg sauce
Boiled capon with
broccoli and white sauce
Mutton cutlets à la Réforme
Sweetbreads
Roast pheasant
Macaroni au gratin
Punch jelly
Pear tartlet

△ THE MENU would vary with the season of the year, although the wealthy could serve out-of-season produce from their hothouses.

△ BY KEEPING grapes on the stem and feeding them from a bottle of water and charcoal they could be kept for up to 3 months.

KITCHENS

OVER THE LAST TWO CENTURIES, kitchen designers have learned how to pack more and more into less and less space. The kitchen of a great house of about 1780 was a place where food was prepared and the servants ate. Food was stored in a separate pantry, a well-ventilated storeroom with shelves of cool marble. Washing dishes and jobs that needed lots of rinsing water, like gutting fish or game, were done in a small scullery, with water coming from a hand pump. By the 1880s the most up-to-date kitchens might have had running cold water from a tap, constant hot water from a tank heated by a range, a gas stove, and a zinc-lined icebox for keeping food cool. Hand-powered gadgets would have included machines for mincing, slicing, and grinding, as well as more specialized jobs like making ice cream, cleaning cutlery, and stoning cherries. In the store cupboards there would have been glass jars of pickles and preserves, made in autumn to last through the winter. There might even have been a few tins of meat or fruit.

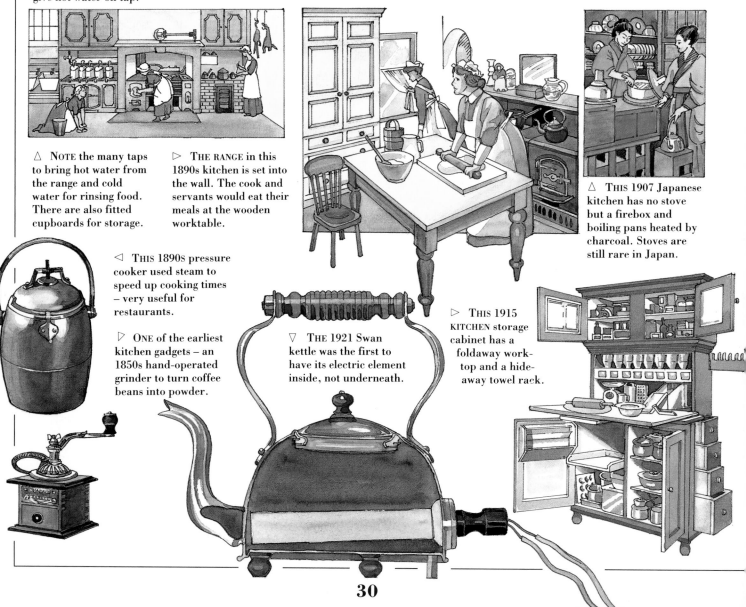

△ THIS GERMAN STOVE of 1784 is wood-burning and has a spit to turn meat and a hood to take away smoke.

▽ THIS STATE-OF-THE-ART KITCHEN, 1821, has a coal-fired iron range heating an oven, hot plates, and a tank to give hot water on tap.

△ NOTE the many taps to bring hot water from the range and cold water for rinsing food. There are also fitted cupboards for storage.

▷ THE RANGE in this 1890s kitchen is set into the wall. The cook and servants would eat their meals at the wooden worktable.

△ THIS 1907 Japanese kitchen has no stove but a firebox and boiling pans heated by charcoal. Stoves are still rare in Japan.

◁ THIS 1890s pressure cooker used steam to speed up cooking times – very useful for restaurants.

▷ ONE of the earliest kitchen gadgets – an 1850s hand-operated grinder to turn coffee beans into powder.

▽ THE 1921 Swan kettle was the first to have its electric element inside, not underneath.

▷ THIS 1915 KITCHEN storage cabinet has a foldaway work-top and a hide-away towel rack.

△ THIS LUXURY
American kitchen of the
1920s has large storage facilities,
including an icebox. The central cabinet
is raised off the floor to keep out ants.

By the 1930s the most modern kitchens
had changed from gas to electricity,
not only for cooking but also to run a
refrigerator, a toaster, and a kettle. By
the 1950s electric mixers, freezers, and
dishwashers were available, though
they were common only in the United
States. Plastic containers and utensils
began to replace tin and enamel ones.
By the 1980s the taste for steel and
shining surfaces was giving way to a
more "natural" look – but the hi-tech
gadgets remained.

◁ BY THE 1920S this
type of solid-fuel stove
was being replaced by
the gas or electric
stove.

▷ AN ELECTRIC
REFRIGERATOR like this
was still very much a
luxury in the 1920s.

◁ MICROWAVE OVENS
like this one first
appeared in the 1970s.
They not only cook
food faster but can also
be used for
reheating and
defrosting.

△ AN AMERICAN
kitchen of the 1950s
with a wall-mounted
oven and a dishwasher.
Colored paints and
plastics were beginning
to be used.

△ THIS 1970S STOVE is
for the real enthusiast.
It combines a large
grill, a double-oven and
six top-burners. It
would be big enough for
a small restaurant.

▷ A 1990S KITCHEN
disguises "hi-tech"
equipment with old-
fashioned farmhouse-
style fittings and decor
using bricks, wood, and
rough tiles.

FARMING

△ OXEN were the main draft-animals in medieval Europe. An acre was originally the area a team could plow in a day.

UNPREDICTABLE WEATHER and crop diseases have always made the farmer's life uncertain, so that throughout history most were inclined to stick to traditional trusted methods rather than run further risks by experimenting. The so-called "Agricultural Revolution" (it actually happened fairly slowly) began in northwest Europe in the seventeenth and eighteenth centuries. As Holland and England prospered on overseas trade, their cities grew too, creating new markets for farmers. This gave them an incentive to risk change in order to grow more produce for sale to the city-dwellers.

△ CROP ROTATION in the Middle Ages left a third of the land uncultivated each year, so that it could recover.

△ THE 18TH-CENTURY "Norfolk rotation" kept all the land in production every year and improved fertility.

▷ THE TRIANGULAR FRAME of the Rotherham plow of the 1730s cut through soil more easily than the old square-framed type.

▽ SYSTEMATIC BREEDING could produce monsters like the Lincolnshire ox of 1790, exhibited by its proud owner in London's Hyde Park.

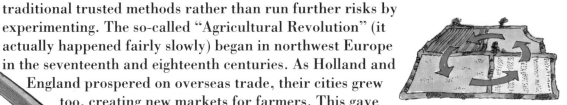

▷ JETHRO TULL'S seed drill (1701) saved seed by dispensing it neatly in rows; but it was too costly for most farmers and unsuitable for use on heavy land.

▽ THIS 1860s MODEL FARM was designed so that the farmer could keep an eye on the farmyard from his house.

▷ THIS WINNOWING MACHINE sped up the task of separating grain from its outer husk.

New methods of making iron cheaply encouraged the invention of new types of farm machinery, and cheap clay pipes made it possible to drain heavy soils. Cheaper bricks meant better buildings to shelter animals and store crops. Enclosing open land with hedges and walls made it possible to control the breeding of livestock and guard against disease. Better roads made it easier to transport chalk, lime, and wastes, like fish, bones, or cloth, to improve the soil.

By the 1880s, railroads, steamships, and refrigeration made it possible to connect the lands of Canada, Argentina, Australia, and New Zealand with the growing cities of Europe, where there was a demand for cheap wheat, canned corned beef, and chilled lamb. This was the beginning of a global marketplace in food. Today, supermarkets buy produce flown in daily from farms in countries as diverse as southern Spain, Israel, and Kenya.

Modern farmers in Europe or North America now have to take account of the tastes and demands of distant markets, as well as the traditional farmers' concerns such as soil and weather conditions and the changing seasons for crops.

△ THIS LATE VICTORIAN FARM has solid brick buildings to keep animals and machinery dry and provide cover for winter work.

▽ MODERN PIGSTIES allow efficient control of feed, light, and ventilation. Concentrating animals in a small space requires strict hygiene standards.

△ A TRADITIONAL Italian farm produced all the family's basic needs but had little surplus to sell.

△ HARSH SCANDINAVIAN winters require large farm buildings to shelter valuable livestock.

△ THE FLAT, FERTILE LAND of the North American prairie is ideal for mechanized farming of grain.

△ MANY SMALL FARMS in New England have become city people's second homes for holidays and weekends.

△ THE SOUTH AMERICAN PRAIRIES have long provided rich grazing for herds of beef cattle for export.

◁ HARVESTING LETTUCE in California. Lettuce comes off the harvester trimmed, wrapped, and boxed for transport.

▷ AT EGG CITY, near Los Angeles, 90,000 chickens consume 250 tons of food and produce one million eggs each day. When a chicken fails to reach its quota it goes to make soup. "Battery-farming" produces cheap food but critics say it is cruel to animals, and that the food is of poor quality.

PRESERVING FOOD

CHEATING THE CUSTOMER

△ ADDING SAND to sugar greatly increased the apparent weight sold over the counter.

△ BREAD was whitened by adding plaster of Paris and bones ground into dust.

△ MILK was easily diluted with unboiled water straight from the pump.

I N 1795 THE FRENCH GOVERNMENT offered 12,000 francs for the invention of a way to store food for use by an army on the march. The prize was won in 1810 by Parisian confectioner Nicolas Appert. His method involved putting food in glass jars, corking them loosely, immersing them in hot water, hammering the corks in tightly, and finally sealing the top airtight. His method was soon applied to tin canisters ("cans") which were much less fragile than glass jars. In 1814 a London firm, Donkin, Hall and Gamble, began to supply the Royal Navy with canned soups and meats to be carried as emergency "medical comforts." A can of their veal and carrots sealed in 1818 was opened in 1938 and found to be perfectly edible. Thanks to the research of the French scientist Louis Pasteur (1822-95), the nature of bacteria – which cause food to go bad – became much better understood.

During the American Civil War (1861-65) canned foods were used to supply armies on a large scale for the first time. In 1868 P.D. Armour opened a giant meat cannery in Chicago to supply the civilian market. Canned meat cost half as much as fresh meat but consumers remained wary of it; the canning process was not always reliable and severe food poisoning could result if cans leaked. After the process was perfected H.J. Heinz launched a wide range of canned goods in America in the 1920s.

△ A WOMAN WORKER in an early frozen-food factory. Frozen foodstuffs have been sold since the 1920s. At first the main product was vegetables but later new foods, like fish sticks, were specially developed for freezing.

In the 1800s the Industrial Revolution led to the rapid growth of towns. This meant that fewer people could grow their own food and they had to buy from stores. There were no laws or food experts to protect them. Unscrupulous storekeepers added brick dust to pepper, used chemicals to make pickles taste spicy, and mixed used tea leaves with fresh ones for resale. In Britain laws to prevent these abuses began in 1860.

△ AIRTIGHT stoneware jars have been used for drinks, honey, mustard, and cheese since Roman times.

▷ IN THE MID-1800s, cheap color printing enabled manufacturers to use bright labels to make tin cans more attractive. Labeling was not intended to inform consumers about the contents so much as to persuade them to buy.

△ THIS EARLY CANNING FACTORY has a simple production line, but very little machinery. Each can has to be sealed by hand. As long as this was so, canned goods remained expensive and beyond the reach of the ordinary person.

△ THE FIRST FOOD product to be sold in cans regularly and in large quantities was corned beef. The main centers of production were the American Midwest and Argentina. Most went for export.

▽ THE PLASTIC PACKING Around these tomatoes is not airtight but allows some gases to pass through. It helps the tomatoes keep for an extra week.

▽ TODAY, treatment with gamma rays kills bacteria. Its use has spread from sterilizing medical equipment to preventing potatoes from sprouting. It may be a cheap way to preserve foods but experts are cautious about its effect on health.

FOOD FROM THE SEA

△ AT FIRST whales were hunted to provide oil, for lamps and later for lard. Today in Japan whale meat is a delicacy.

DEEP-SEA FISHING was a well-organized industry off the coasts of Europe by the Middle Ages. Catches were salted, dried, or pickled so that they could be stored, carried, and sold far inland. By the sixteenth century large fleets were crossing the Atlantic to exploit rich fishing grounds off Newfoundland. Disputes over fishing rights were a cause of wars between Britain and Holland in the 1650s. The invention of steam power and refrigeration during the nineteenth century enabled ships to operate even farther from home waters. Today electronic devices enable fleets to trace and track shoals of fish, saving much time and fuel. More than 5,000,000 people are employed in fishing worldwide, notably from Japan, Russia, China, and the United States. The most commonly caught fish are cod, plaice, sole, and haddock, which are found in deep water, and herring and tuna, which are found near the surface.

△ INUIT PEOPLES fish using harpoons, lines, or nets. Storage is no problem with so much ice around to freeze the catch.

△ "FISHWIVES" used to work at the dockside in the last century, gutting the fresh catch and packing the fish into barrels with salt to preserve it.

△ MODERN FISH FARMS raise fish as a "crop" – from egg to market. The most common "crops" are carp, trout, salmon, and catfish.

▽ DIP NETS hang over a ship's side on a frame which is pulled up to bring in the catch.

△ TODAY factory ships catch the fish, then prepare, freeze, and pack it on board, while the ship is still at sea.

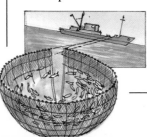
◁ THE PURSE SEINE NET is used to surround shoals of fish in open sea. When drawn tight it makes a trap.

▽ ▷ DRIFT NETS drift with the tides and are up to 60 mi long. They are used far out at sea.

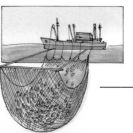

▷ AN OPEN-AIR MARKET in England in about 1870. Most of the produce would be fresh fruit, vegetables, and eggs from local farms. Note the use of barrels and wicker baskets for transport and display. The covered stall in the center sold ice cream, served in glasses.

SHOPPING

BEFORE THE COMING OF THE RAILROADS and the invention of canning, most foodstuffs had a short "shelf life" and had to be bought fresh from markets or stores near the place where they were produced. Grocers bought butter, bacon, or sugar in bulk and weighed out what each customer wanted. This made it easy to cheat them by giving short weight or adding harmful chemicals to "improve" the flavor (see page 34). "Honest John" Horniman began a retailing revolution in London in the 1830s by offering customers a sealed packet guaranteed to hold four ounces of pure tea. In the 1870s grocer Thomas Lipton made his fortune by selling only those goods that the housewife had to buy every week. By buying huge quantities he was able to keep prices low, and so his shop was extremely popular.

△ DISPLAYS OF MEAT and poultry were often more eye-catching than hygienic.

▽ SELF-SERVICE supermarkets save on labor and encourage "impulse buying." They first appeared in the United States in the 1940s.

▽ A GROCER'S SHOP of 1915 with shelves of packaged goods and a bacon-slicing machine.

An English Christmas pudding.

CHRISTMAS AROUND EUROPE

△ BRITAIN: Turkey with cranberry sauce; Christmas pudding and brandy butter.

△ DENMARK: Duck or goose stuffed with fruit; rice pudding topped with cinnamon.

△ FRANCE: Oysters; goose-liver pâté; turkey with white wine and champagne; cheeses.

△ IRELAND: Turkey and ham are eaten on Christmas Day itself.

△ GERMANY: Carp or herring on Christmas Eve; roast goose on Christmas Day.

△ SPAIN: Roast lamb on Christmas Eve; shellfish; turkey; suckling pig; sherry.

△ NETHERLANDS: Rabbit, venison, or game served on Christmas Day.

△ PORTUGAL: Baccalao (dried and salted codfish); very sweet port wine.

△ BELGIUM: Veal sausage stuffed with truffles; wild boar; traditional cake; wine.

△ GREECE: Turkey served with wine.

△ LUXEMBOURG: Blood sausage; apples; sparkling local wine.

△ ITALY: Steamed cod or bass, served with white wine, on Christmas Eve.

CELEBRATION

CELEBRATING FAMILY EVENTS often involves preparing and eating special food. A cake is the centerpiece of many birthday or wedding meals. Every guest receives a small piece of it, to symbolize sharing the happiness of the day. The birth of a baby, or christening or naming ceremony, is another time when special food may be shared. When people in Scotland move into a new house, their neighbors often bring a gift of bread and salt, which traditionally represent the basic foodstuffs that no household should be without. Although a funeral is a sad time, family and friends may celebrate the end of a person's life with a gathering involving eating, drinking, and sometimes even dancing.

◁ THE LANGAR (free kitchen) was founded by the Sikhs' first guru (teacher) to show his followers they must share food as equals. Worshipers eat at the langar after their weekly service.

△ MUSLIMS leading a sheep for the feast after Ramadan.

◁ A JEWISH CUSTOM is for candles to be lit by the mother of a family at the start of the Friday-evening Shabbat meal.

◁ JAPANESE FAMILIES mark New Year with *O-sechi ryori* – mixed cold dishes of lucky red beans and rice; rice-cakes; pickles and vegetables.

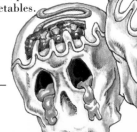

△ THE AMERICAN FEAST of Thanksgiving commemorates the first English settlers who, in 1621, thanked God for surviving a year in the wilderness. It only became a national holiday in the 1860s.

Different religious customs also involve eating special kinds of foods, feasting, or fasting. For example, at the festival of Passover, Jewish families eat a special meal called a *seder*. They drink four cups of wine and eat raw vegetables, bitter herbs, and unleavened bread – symbolic reminders of the hard journey through the desert made by the Jews when they escaped from Egypt in ancient times. Judaism and other religions have strict rules about how food is prepared.

△ A MUSLIM FAMILY FEAST. During the month of Ramadan, Muslims fast all through daylight hours. The end of the fast is celebrated with a feast. Another feast takes place at the time of the annual pilgrimage to Mecca.

◁ IN MEXICO the spirits of the ancestors are welcomed back each year on The Day of the Dead. Candy in the shape of skulls and skeletons is made of thick sugar and marzipan.

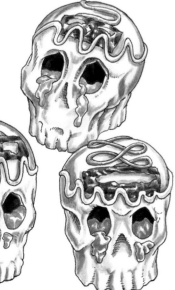

Other celebrations have their origins in the farming calendar. In the past most people survived on what their own village could grow. At the time of planting, in the spring, they might have special ceremonies to ask the gods to watch over their crops and protect them from disease and bad weather. At harvest, they celebrated the gathering-in of the winter's food supply. The Roman goddess of the harvest was Ceres. Her name gives us the English word "cereal."

◁ THE TIERED WEDDING CAKE was invented by a City of London baker in the eighteenth century. He wanted to make something different but could not think of anything until he looked up to see the tiered steeple of St. Bride's church.

Wheat.

Maize. Millet.

Sorghum.

Pasta.

STAPLE FOODS

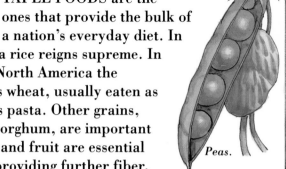
Peas.

STAPLE FOODS are the ones that provide the bulk of a nation's everyday diet. In eastern Asia rice reigns supreme. In Europe and North America the essential crop is wheat, usually eaten as bread, but also as pasta. Other grains, such as millet and sorghum, are important in Africa. Vegetables and fruit are essential for a balanced diet, providing further fiber, vitamins, and a variety of textures and flavors. They can usually be grown in small quantities and therefore enable individual families to supplement what they buy from the professional farmer.

Bread.

△ BREAD in various forms has been made for 12,000 years. A basic difference is between flat (pita) and raised varieties.

△ PULSES, such as lentils, and tubers, like potatoes, are now recognized as good fiber-providers for healthy digestion.

Beehive.

Brussels sprouts.

◁ ▽ VEGETABLES are eaten as leaves, stems, pods, roots, and seeds. They provide both bulk and essential vitamins.

Onions.

Asparagus.

Spinach.

Cabbage.

Cherries.

Sugar beet.

Sugarcane.

▷ △ HONEY was the main sweetener in cold climates until sugar began to be imported.

Fig.

Bananas.

▷ A GREAT VARIETY of fruit grows in the tropics.

Sweet pepper. Eggplant.

△ EGGPLANTS, sweet peppers, and onions are basic ingredients for the dishes of the Middle East, giving both fiber and flavor.

Lychee.

As societies become wealthier, people tend to eat less of the most basic foods and increase the variety in their diet, for instance by eating more expensive foods imported from other countries. This can be perfectly healthy. But if they reject basic foodstuffs like bread, rice, or root vegetables as "boring," this can lead to digestion problems and other results of an unbalanced diet. In a poor country bad weather or a crop disease that causes a harvest failure of the staple foodstuff can mean the possibility of starvation.

Tea.

◁ AN EARLY ENGRAVING of a still for distilling strong alcoholic spirits – from Salerno, Italy around 1480.

▷ COFFEE, tea, and cocoa are all native to tropical regions but are consumed daily throughout the world.

Coffee.

Cocoa beans.

STARVATION

ALTHOUGH HUNTER-GATHERER PEOPLES live close to the margin of survival all the time, their risk of starvation is diminished by the variety of food sources they can fall back on. Settled peoples, and especially those who have come to depend on a single crop, are far more vulnerable to mass famine if that crop fails. Drought, floods, disease, and insects have been the most common causes of crop destruction. Ancient empires built huge granaries and water control systems to try to cope with these dangers. Warfare has been just as destructive as these environmental problems. Soldiers destroy crops and livestock, farmers flee, and the land is left untended. Unless outsiders help, famine must follow and with it usually comes disease. More people will die, and this reduces the farm labor-force even more.

Today the United Nations, supported by organizations like OXFAM, UNICEF, and Save the Children, works to bring emergency food supplies to famine-stricken areas. But all these agencies know that what poor countries really need is peace and security so that, with technical assistance, their people can grow their own food and sell what they don't need at a fair price.

△ THE OLD TESTAMENT records how ancient Egypt was plagued by locusts which ate all the crops.

▽ VICTORIAN CHARITIES set up "soup kitchens" in slum areas to provide the poor with a free meal.

△ DURING the Middle Ages giving charity to beggars was seen as a basic duty of all Christians. Monasteries took care of many old people and orphans.

▽ THE GREAT IRISH FAMINE of the 1840s was caused by a blight which destroyed the essential potato crop three years running. The British government issued rations, but the effort was too little and too late to prevent more than a million deaths and mass immigration abroad.

△ SOIL EROSION and drought brought poverty to America's farmlands in the 1930s.

▷ KWASHIORKOR, caused by acute lack of protein, leads to an accumulation of fluids that make the sufferer look bloated.

▷ FAMINES in war-torn areas like eastern Africa have led to major relief efforts by international agencies.

◁ MARASMUS is caused by lack of calories as well as lack of protein. Body weight may fall to half its normal level.

△ IN MANY DEVELOPING COUNTRIES farmers have to rely on cash crops like tobacco for their income. Sudden price changes can push them into deep debt.

FAST FOOD

EATING "FAST FOOD" may be more common than ever before, but it is nothing new. Hot noodles could be eaten at wayside stalls in the cities of ancient China. In 12th-century Seville the market supervisor issued regulations that banned stall-holders from selling fritters using leftover ingredients from the previous day. In London at the same time there were riverside cookshops where hot meals could be bought 24 hours a day.

◁ JAPANESE boxed lunch – *O-bento* – can be bought at most railroad stations.

△ *O-BENTO* contain cold snacks of rice, fish, pickles, and omelet. Throwaway chopsticks are also provided. Hard-working businessmen eat boxed lunches at their desk.

△ THE HAMBURGER was invented in the port of Hamburg and brought to America by German immigrants in the 1850s. American law requires it to be made of pure beef.

▽ IN THE MIDDLE EAST flat loaves of unleavened bread are split to make "pockets" filled with meat, fish, and fresh salad.

▷ A CONVEYER-BELT is used to serve *sushi* – neat patties of vinegared rice topped with raw fish – at this hi-tech Japanese lunch counter.

Coffee and pie stalls were popular in London in the 1840s. Fish-and-chip shops grew with the railroads, which brought fresh fish from the coast overnight. The popularity of fast food and "take-out" meals can be largely explained by the trend of smaller families and greater mobility in the daily lives of city-dwellers. In providing such food as hamburgers, pizzas, or fried chicken, great care is taken by the manufacturers over the quality and mixture of ingredients, first to ensure the customer's health, but also because people expect all the portions to be exactly the same.

▽ THESE SNACKS come from a street stall in Thailand, in handy bite-sized chunks. Thai food is very spicy and often hot as well.

THE FUTURE

THE SEABED is rich in decayed animal and vegetable matter which could be used to fertilize undersea crops. But in most places, light – essential for growth – does not penetrate below 160 feet (50m); if ways could be found to bring this seabed fertilizer nearer the surface, then underwater "deserts" could be turned into ocean "prairies." Already plants like giant kelp, which grows 3 feet ($\frac{1}{2}$ m) a day and can reach 230 feet (70 m) in height, are being used to feed cattle. At the other end of the scale are tiny spirulina, freshwater algae, being raised commercially in Mexico and California. Genetic engineering and simulating cross-breeding programs on a computer offer the possibility of "designing" plants which are able to withstand drought and disease. And the possibility of self-supporting space stations means that even the sky is no longer the limit.

△ SPIRULINA, a type of algae, magnified 400 times. Grown in lakes, it yields 40 percent more protein than meat.

△ A SPACE STATION might use solar power to recycle human wastes, like water and carbon dioxide, to grow food in outer space.

▽ AN IMPRESSION of a seabed farm of the future, with a food processing plant, and workers arriving by shuttle.

△ THIS "TOBEAN" is a hybrid of a French bean and a tobacco plant, produced by genetic engineering in a laboratory. Experiments like this may lead to new "superplants," able to survive in inhospitable areas of the world.

TIMELINE

Coconut

B.C.
3000 Sugar-making first recorded in India. Date-palm first cultivated in the Middle East.
c.1750 Law code of Hammurabi of Babylon controls quality standards of beer.

Harvesting in Ancient Egypt

A.D.
100 Emperor Trajan establishes Rome's first guild of professional bakers.
c.300 Earliest manuscript of the recipe book said to be by the Roman gourmet, Apicius.

Roman butcher

851 Porcelain drinking bowls in use in China.
c.1000 Coffee begins to be used as a medicine in the Middle East, used to combat drowsiness.
c.1200 Sugared almonds, the first known candy, recorded in France.
1205 First record of cider being made in Norfolk, England.

1319 First record of sugar being imported to London.
1493 Columbus introduces sugarcane to the Americas. The plant originally came from India.
1495 First record of Scotch whisky.
1519 In Mexico, Montezuma offers the Spanish invader Cortes *xocolatl* (chocolate) to drink.
1521 Cocoa beans brought from the Americas to Spain.
1523 Tomato plants brought from the Americas to Europe.
1530 First mention of corks to seal bottles.
1544 London's first sugar refineries established.
c.1550 Chemical "refrigeration" process using saltpeter invented in Rome for chilling wine.
1554 First public coffee-house opened in Istanbul.
1573 First record of potatoes being grown in Europe. At first they are grown as ornamental plants. Some people think the potatoes are poisonous.
1587 First record of marmalade and Brussels sprouts.
1609 Dutch begin importation of tea from China to Europe.
1620s Last recorded deaths from famine in England.
1621 Pilgrim fathers celebrate the first

Distilling alcohol, 1480

Thanksgiving dinner in Massachusetts.
c.1625 First dairy herd established in North America.
1633 First record of bananas in England (regular imports begin in 1884).

Chinese teahouse

1657 First Chocolate House opens in London. At first people drink chocolate without sugar – sometimes it is flavored with spices.
1670 A Sicilian opens the first ice-cream parlor in Paris.
1680 First record of a pressure cooker, invented by the French scientist Denis Papin in London.
1701 Englishman Jethro Tull invents the seed-drill.
c.1730 First record of jam-making in the UK.
1741 First carbonated mineral-water prepared by Dr Brownrigg of Cumberland, England.
1747 The German chemist, Marggraf, experiments with ways to extract sugar from beet.
1760 Licorice candy first sold by George Dunhill of Yorkshire, England.
1762 Fourth Earl of Sandwich, unwilling to leave the gambling table, calls for a snack of meat between two slices of bread, thereby inventing the sandwich.

1765 First restaurant established in Paris by a soup-seller called Boulanger, who names his special soups "Restaurants," meaning restoratives, or potions to make people feel better.
1785 Soda water manufactured by Rawlings of London.
1786 First threshing-machine devised by Scotsman Andrew Meikle.
1788 Grapevines first planted in Australia.
1795 A method of preserving vegetables by hot air dehydration is invented in France.
1802 The world's first sugar-beet factory opens in Silesia in Eastern Europe.
1804 First restaurant guide published, listing 500 eating-places in Paris.

Pita bread

1806 American Benjamin Rumford invents the coffee-percolator.
1808 Ransome's of Ipswich, England, produce the first all-iron plow.

Scullery maid, 19th century

1812 First canned food manufactured in London by Donkin, Hall & Gamble.
1815 First cheese factory established in Switzerland. Carr's of Carlisle, England, open the world's first biscuit factory.
1819 First canned sardines become available in Nantes, France. First eating chocolate manufactured in Switzerland. It is dark-colored and bitter to taste.

Japanese candy

1820 Scientist Friedrich Accum of Hanover publishes his pioneering study of food adulteration.
1830s Tea in packets first sold in London.
1831 American Cyrus McCormick perfects a horse-drawn reaper.
1837 Worcester sauce first manufactured by Lea & Perrins using a secret combination of spices. The first public demonstration of a gas cooker is given in the UK.
1841 Master chef Alexis Soyer pioneers gas-cooking at the Reform Club in London.
1845 First self-rising flour made in Bristol,

Cardamom

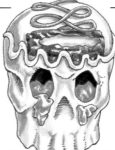

African snail

England. Eliza Acton's book *Modern Cookery* pioneers systematic, detailed descriptions of recipes.
1845–7 Failure of the Irish potato crop causes major famine.
1847 First ring doughnuts made in Camden, Maine. The Vegetarian Society of England is formed. Evaporated milk is patented in the UK.
1848 Chewing-gum first manufactured, in Bangor, Maine.
1850 Gas stoves begin to come on general sale to the public in the UK. First potato chips made in Saratoga Springs, New York. First candy bar – Fry's Cream Stick – made in Bristol, England.
1851 First ice-cream factory, Baltimore, Maryland.
1854 During the Crimean War, Alexis Soyer designs standard army field stove, which remains the basic design used by the army for the next century.
1855 Powdered milk is patented in the UK.
1859 Publication of *Mrs Beeton's Book of Household Management.*
1860 UK becomes the first country to pass general laws against the adulteration of food and drink.
1867 First regular day-school meals introduced in Paris.
1869 Margarine is invented by a Frenchman but patented in the UK.
1870s The first factory production of sausages takes place in the UK.
1875 First canned baked beans produced

in Maine.
1877 First cargo of refrigerated meat is shipped from Argentina to Europe.
1878 First cube sugar produced by Henry Tate, in London.
1879 Discovery of saccharin at Johns Hopkins University. First use of bottles to deliver milk, New York.
1885 First self-service cafe opens in New York. First cream crackers manufactured in Dublin by Wm. Jacob.
1886 Coca-Cola launched in Georgia, as an "Esteemed Brain Tonic and Intellectual Beverage." Paper drinking-straws first sold in Washington, D.C.
1890 The first aluminum saucepan is produced in Cleveland, Ohio. First beverage

Pressure cooker, 1890s

vending machines are installed in factories in Birmingham, England.
1892 First Thermos flask is produced in Cambridge, England.
1893 William Wrigley sells Juicy Fruit gum in America. First electric toaster manufactured in Chelmsford, England. First breakfast cereal,

Shredded Wheat, manufactured in Denver, Colorado.
1894 First electric kettle goes on sale in the UK.
1896 First chop-suey (Chinese for "bits and pieces") sold in New York. First ice-cream cone is made in New Jersey. Before this, ices were only available in shaped blocks.
1898 Corn flakes promoted as a vegetarian health-food by Dr Wm Kellogg of Michigan.
1902 Marmite first manufactured in

Indian candy peddler

Burton-on-Trent, England.
1906 Free school meals for poor children are introduced in the UK. New Zealand pioneers cultivation of the kiwi fruit (from China). Instant coffee – coffee in soluble form – invented by Mr G Washington, an Englishman living in Guatemala.
1908 First paper cups become available in New York.
1909 The first H.J. Heinz canned food factory is established in the UK.
1913 First domestic refrigerators go on sale in Chicago. Chips first manufactured in the UK.
1922 First canned baby-food is manufactured in Rochester, New York.

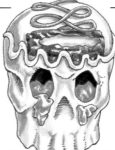

Mexican sugar skull

1928 Bubble gum goes on sale in America.
1930 First frozen food goes on sale in Massachusetts. First large-scale, self-service supermarket opens on Long Island, New York.
1932 First Mars Bar is manufactured in Slough, England.
1933 Thermostatic controls are introduced in the UK to give more accurate temperature control in electric ovens.
1934 First automatic tea-maker, the "Teasmade" is produced by Goblin of Leatherhead, Surrey, UK.

1920s refrigerator

1938 Instant coffee powder perfected by Nestlé of Switzerland. Self-propelled combine-harvester introduced in the United States.

Harvesting lettuce in California

1945 United Nations founds the Food & Agriculture Organization (FAO) at its first specialized agency. First patent for a microwave oven is registered in Massachusetts.
1946 "Espresso" coffee-machine, using steam from boiling water forced through coffee powder, is invented in Italy.
1948 Kenwood introduces the electrically powered food mixer in America. United Nations establishes World Health Organization (WHO).
1950s Chinese take-out counters and coffee-bars begin to appear.
1955 Non-stick saucepans first sold in Paris.
1960s Indian restaurants begin to appear. Growing popularity of instant powdered coffee and frozen convenience foods.
1967 Weight Watchers slimming clubs are introduced from America to the UK.
1970s Growing popularity of yogurts and gyros.
1972 Britain's first McDonald's opens in London.
1980s Introduction of bar-coding. Growing popularity of organic foods, bottled mineral water, and microwave ovens.
1985 "Band Aid" concert raises cash to relieve Ethiopian famine.
1991 McDonald's opens a branch in Moscow.

GLOSSARY

Boar A wild pig.

Canapé A party snack made of bread or pastry with a savory topping.

Cassava A tropical plant, the roots of which can be ground up to make flour.

Casserole A deep, covered dish for baking and serving food.

Caviar Pickled eggs of the sturgeon, a large fish found in the Caspian Sea.

Chop suey Chinese dish consisting of small pieces of meat fried with bean sprouts, rice, and vegetables.

Couscous Traditional North African dish made from crushed wheat or semolina steamed over broth and served with fruit or meat added in.

Cuisine A style of cooking.

Deficiency disease Illness caused by lack of a vital element in the diet.

Dehydration Method of removing water from something in order to preserve it.

Fasting Giving up food, usually for religious reasons.

Fermentation Chemical process through which a complex substance is broken down into simpler substances. For example, sugar turning into alcohol.

Fritter A small, flat piece of fried batter containing fruit or meat.

Fungi Types of nonflowering plants, without roots, stems, or leaves, such as mushrooms or truffles.

Game Wild animals or birds hunted for food, such as hares and pheasants.

Ghee Butter, heated to produce a clear liquid oil, used for cooking in India.

Goulash Hungarian stew of meat and vegetables, highly seasoned with paprika.

Granary A store-house for grain.

Horticulture The art of cultivating vegetables and fruit.

Husk Dry outside covering of a fruit or seed.

Kebab A Middle Eastern dish of small pieces of meat, onion, peppers, etc., grilled on skewers.

Kedgeree Dish made of rice, fish, and hard-boiled eggs.

Livery Uniform worn by a servant.

Marinade Mixture of oil, wine, vinegar, herbs, etc. used to soak meat or fish to enrich its flavor and make it softer before cooking.

Mead An alcoholic drink made of fermented honey and water.

Moussaka A Greek or Turkish dish made with minced meat and eggplants.

Mutton The meat from a mature sheep. Meat from younger animals is known as "lamb".

Neanderthal People who lived in Europe in the "Old Stone Age," when flint tools were used but farming had not begun.

Neolithic "New Stone Age"; period before the general use of metals but after the domestication of animals and development of agriculture.

Nomads Peoples who have no fixed home, usually because they care for herds of livestock which are constantly moved in search of fresh grazing.

Offal Edible internal parts of an animal (heart, liver, kidneys).

Okra Green pod of a West African plant, eaten in soups and stews.

Palatable Pleasant to eat.

Pasta Dough-mixture of wheat flour and water dried into a variety of shapes (for example, macaroni, spaghetti, lasagne, ravioli).

Pimiento A sweet pepper.

Plantain A fruit similar to a banana, used in Caribbean cooking.

Pulses Edible seeds of podded plants, such as peas, beans, lentils.

Quern stones Two flat stones used for grinding corn and other grains to make flour.

Range A large stove, usually made of cast iron, with a coal or gas fire to heat the oven and top plates.

Ratatouille French vegetable stew of tomatoes, zucchini, eggplants, peppers and onions.

Sashimi Japanese dish of raw fish, thinly sliced and served with soy sauce and other flavorings.

Sauerkraut A German dish of chopped pickled cabbage. *Sauer* means "sour" and *kraut* means "cabbage."

Scullery Kitchen backroom used for washing dishes and other messy jobs.

Scurvy Disease caused by lack of vitamin C in the diet.

Stock Flavored liquid prepared by boiling meat, fish or vegetables with herbs and spices; stock is used to make stews, soups, and sauces.

Tortilla Flat cake made from maize flour and eaten hot or cold.

Truffle Richly flavored fungus that grows underground.

Tuber Thick rounded root or underground stem (for example, a potato).

Tundra Region of the Arctic where the soil is always frozen.

Unscrupulous Describes a person who has no principles and cannot be trusted.

Veal The meat from a calf.

Vegan Strict vegetarian who will not eat any animal products (for example, eggs).

Venison The meat from a deer.

Viper A poisonous snake.

Zinc A white-colored metal that does not rust.

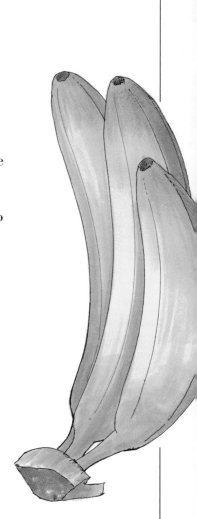

INDEX

PRINTED IN BELGIUM BY
proost
INTERNATIONAL BOOK PRODUCTION

STAR WARS

Illustrated by Art Mawhinney

pi kids
phoenix international publications, inc.

Look and

It's the day of the big Boonta
Eve Podrace on Tatooine! Sebulba
is the favorite, but young Anakin
Skywalker zooms ahead.

While Anakin makes his move,
search the scene for these racers
and their fans:

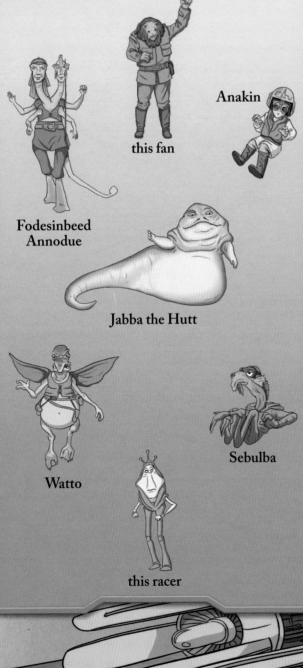

Anakin

this fan

Fodesinbeed
Annodue

Jabba the Hutt

Watto

Sebulba

this racer

Senator Amidala has been attacked! The brave Jedi Knights Anakin Skywalker and Obi-Wan Kenobi chase the senator's attacker through the skies of Coruscant.

Help the Jedi Knights search for the assassin and these other flying things:

GALAXIES OPERA

DEX'S

Supreme Chancellor Palpatine has been captured by the evil General Grievous! Obi-Wan Kenobi and Anakin Skywalker must blast their way through a blockade of spaceships to save the Supreme Chancellor.

First find the Jedi Knights, then help them avoid enemy fire by spotting these ships:

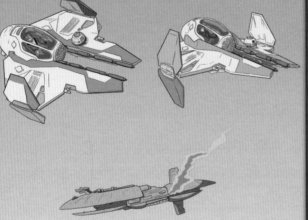

The evil Empire has taken over the galaxy. Luckily, the rebels have a new hope—Luke Skywalker. Now they just need a spaceship!

Search the Cantina on Tatooine for these pirates, smugglers, and other ne'er-do-wells. Is one of them the pilot Luke is looking for?

Greedo

Han Solo

this musician

Chewbacca

this customer

this smuggler

this alien

Han, Chewie, and Princess Leia need somewhere to hide from the evil Darth Vader. Cloud City, run by Han's old friend Lando Calrissian, seems like the perfect place!

But something isn't right for our heroes. Search the scene for these hidden menaces:

Han Solo is in the clutches of the slimy gangster Jabba the Hutt. Luckily Han has powerful friends. Luke Skywalker has a message for Jabba—free Han, or else!

While Jabba considers Luke's offer, search Jabba's shindig for these party guests:

this bounty hunter

this party guest

Chewbacca

Han Solo

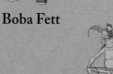

Boba Fett

Luke Skywalker

this party guest

Salacious B. Crumb

Years after the battle of Endor, the distant desert planet Jakku is filled with wrecked ships, busted droids, and other junk. But if you look hard enough, you might just find something great!

Scavenge the desert for all these things:

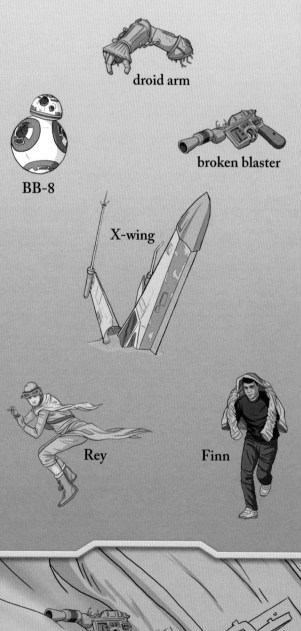

droid arm

BB-8

broken blaster

X-wing

Rey

Finn

Rey is a skilled desert scavenger. She looks through old junk and finds good, usable parts.

As Rey trades in her latest haul for something to eat, look around the trading post for these food-related items:

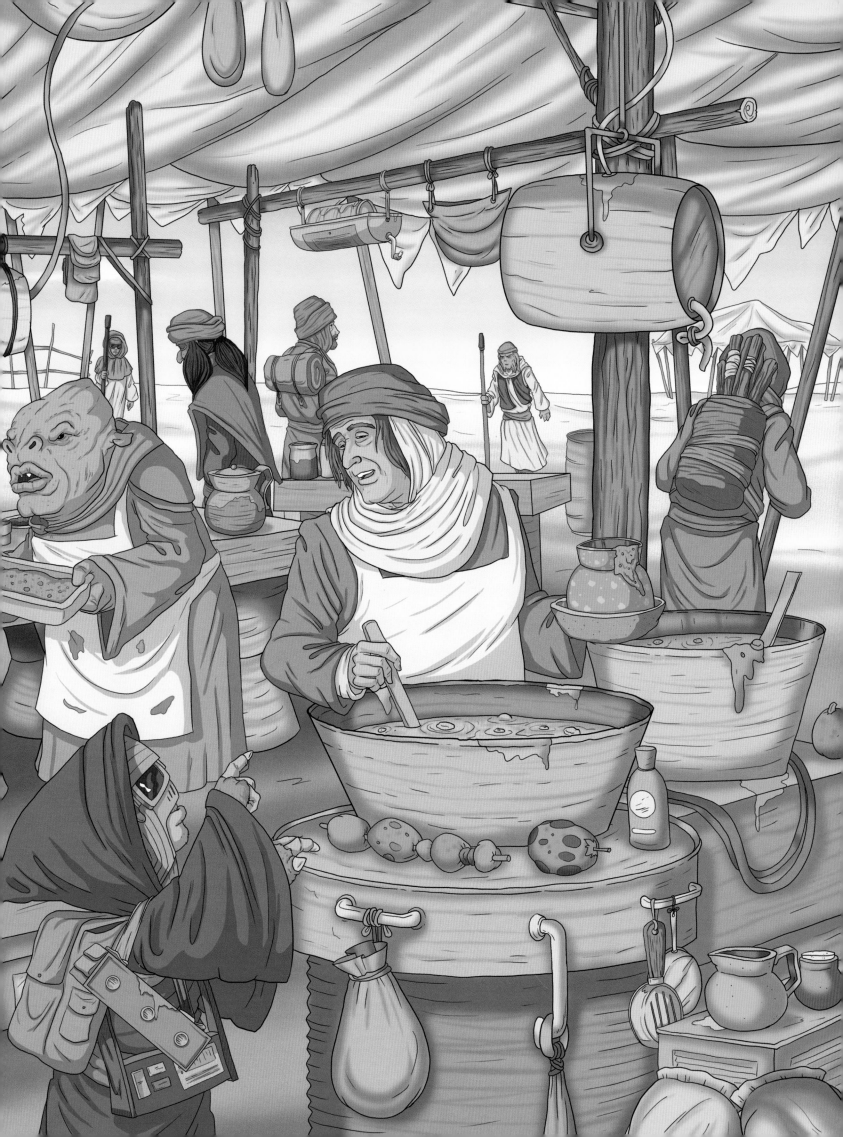

Most spectators put their credits on Sebulba to win, but Anakin has his supporters. Hurry back to the podrace and find fans holding signs that spell A-N-A-K-I-N!

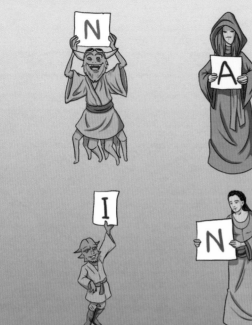

There's plenty to do on Coruscant. Go back to the big city and search for these places:

the Galaxies Opera House

Dex's Diner

the Snapping Septoid

the Vos Gesal Hotel

the Outlander Club

Return to the battle against General Grievous and search for 10 buzz droids, like these:

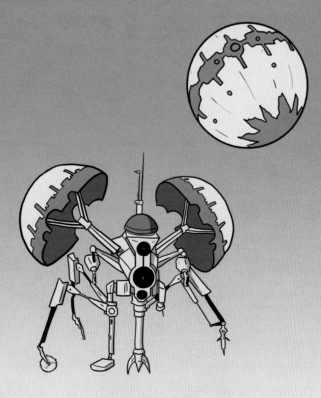

Droids aren't allowed in the Cantina, but some snuck in! Go back to the Cantina and find them. These are the droids you're looking for:

Go back to Cloud City and search the skies for clouds that look like:

Yoda

Darth Vader

a lightsaber

C-3PO

R2-D2

Dance back to Jabba's palace party to find these members of the Max Rebo Band:

Sy Snootles

Ak-rev

Joh Yowza

Lyn Me

Max Rebo

Rystáll Sant

The Jakku desert is a rough place to live, but it's perfect for *some*. Head back to Jakku to find these desert dwellers:

Need a snack? Travel back to the Trading Post on Jakku and trade in these items for some food:

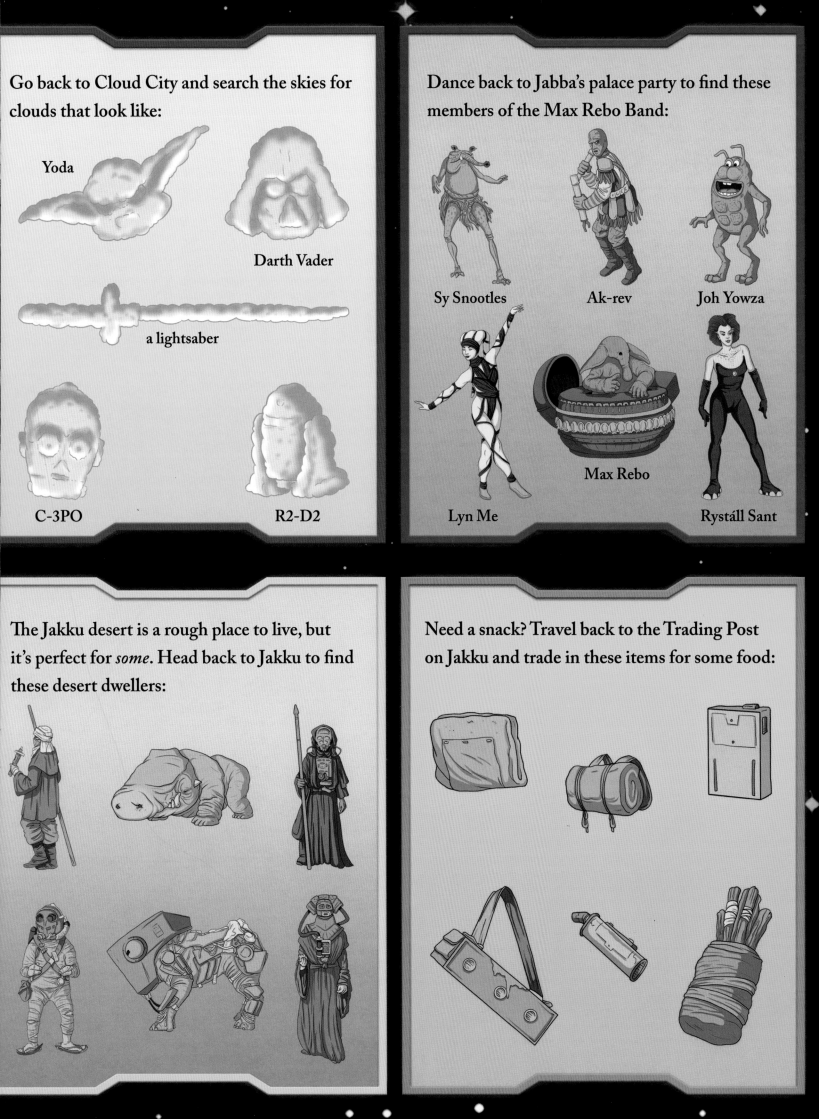